JOSH ALLEN

SUPERSTAR QUARTERBACK

BY TED COLEMAN

Book design by Jake Nordby
Cover design by Jake Slavik

Photographs ©: Brian Blanco/AP Images, cover, 1; Don Wright/AP Images, 4, 6; Shannon Broderick/AP Images, 8; Eli Lucero/The Herald Journal/AP Images, 11; Ben Liebenberg/AP Images, 12; Jeffrey T. Barnes/AP Images, 14, 19; Carlos Gonzalez/ZUMA Press/Newscom, 17; Bill Kostroun/AP Images, 20; Michael Ainsworth/AP Images, 22; Ryan Kang/AP Images, 24, 27 (bottom); Greg Trott/AP Images, 26; Shutterstock Images, 27 (top); Red Line Editorial, 29; Cooper Neill/AP Images, 30

Press Box Books, an imprint of Press Room Editions.

Library of Congress Control Number: 2020901599

ISBN
978-1-63494-208-9 (library bound)
978-1-63494-226-3 (paperback)
978-1-63494-244-7 (epub)
978-1-63494-262-1 (hosted ebook)

Distributed by North Star Editions, Inc.
2297 Waters Drive
Mendota Heights, MN 55120
www.northstareditions.com

Printed in the United States of America
082020

About the Author

Ted Coleman is a sportswriter who lives in Louisville, Kentucky.

TABLE OF CONTENTS

1 NERVES OF STEEL

Josh Allen dropped back to pass. He looked over his options. Soon he was hit by two Pittsburgh Steelers defenders and sacked. On second down, the Buffalo Bills quarterback threw deep for John Brown, but the pass fell incomplete.

Still, Allen didn't surrender. On third down, he used his other dynamic weapon: his legs. He took off running for a 12-yard gain. Then on fourth down, he completed a big 10-yard pass to Brown for the first down.

As the Steelers learned in 2019, Josh Allen is always a threat to run.

Allen and Tyler Kroft celebrate their huge touchdown against Pittsburgh.

That was Allen. It wasn't always pretty. But he found a way to make a play.

Allen knew the stakes that night in 2019. A playoff spot was on the line. For the Bills, the playoffs were a rare achievement. To get it done, they had to win under the lights on *Sunday Night Football* in Pittsburgh.

The game was tied 10–10 in the fourth quarter. Buffalo had the ball on its own 30.

That was when Allen uncorked a deep ball. He hit Brown on the left sideline for a 40-yard gain. The drive took the Bills inside the Pittsburgh 20. Allen faced another key third down. Spotting Tyler Kroft in the end zone, Allen fired a bullet of a pass for a touchdown.

The Bills hung on to win 17–10. It was their 10th victory of the season. They hadn't won that many games in a season in 20 years. And they clinched a playoff spot.

Allen was a surprise top draft pick to many. He came out of a small college. But he showed he belonged in the National Football League (NFL). Bills fans were happy to have him.

RARE WIN IN PITTSBURGH

The Bills and Steelers have been playing each other since 1970. And usually the Steelers have come out on top. The Bills' win in 2019 was just their third victory in 12 games in Pittsburgh. And it was their first since January 1993.

2 STRONG ROOTS

Josh Allen was born May 21, 1996, in Firebaugh, California. He grew up on a 3,000-acre cotton farm. Farming was the family business. But Josh dreamed of being a pro football player.

He had the skills for it. He was so talented that he could have transferred to a bigger high school to get more attention from bigger colleges. But Josh opted to stay in his hometown.

Josh dreamed of playing college football at nearby Fresno State. But the

Josh eventually found a home for himself in Wyoming.

Bulldogs didn't offer him a scholarship. In fact, no schools did.

That didn't faze Josh. He knew he could play college football. So he enrolled at a nearby junior college, hoping to get the attention of a major college program. In his first season he threw for 2,055 yards and 26 touchdowns. He also ran for 660 yards and 10 touchdowns. Josh thought that might convince Fresno State. But he was rejected again.

Instead of giving up, Josh wrote an email. He added a link to a video of his highlights. Josh sent the email to every head coach, offensive or defensive

FUTURE FARMER?

Football was not Josh's only high school activity. He was active in the Future Farmers of America. He was a nationally recognized student in the field of grain harvesting. Josh and his brother Todd also helped on the family farm. They learned to chop cotton and also pulled weeds by hand.

Josh uses his leaping ability to score a touchdown against Utah State in 2017.

coordinator, and quarterbacks coach in college football's top division. Only a few wrote back. Wyoming was one of two schools that offered him a scholarship. Josh accepted it.

Josh's first season in Wyoming in 2015 came to a sudden end when he broke his

collarbone after two games. He won the starting job in 2016 and threw for 3,203 yards and 28 touchdowns. However, he also threw 15 interceptions. He cut that number down to just six in 2017.

His last game for Wyoming was the Famous Idaho Potato Bowl. The Cowboys beat Central Michigan 37-14. Shortly afterward, Josh announced he was skipping his senior season to enter the 2018 NFL Draft.

Josh began preparing for the NFL Combine. Scouts loved his arm strength, accuracy, and running ability. He also had good size and speed. Suddenly, the kid who couldn't get a scholarship was headed to the NFL.

Josh (2) demonstrates his athletic ability at the NFL Combine.

3 BUFFALO BOUND

Allen was considered one of the top players available in the draft. Two quarterbacks went off the board in the first three picks. The Buffalo Bills had the 12th pick, and they wanted a quarterback too. But they worried Allen wouldn't last that long. The Bills traded up just so they could get Allen at No. 7.

Allen was clearly Buffalo's quarterback of the future. And the future arrived quickly. Allen got his first chance to play in Week 1. He came off the bench and

Allen got right to work at his first Bills training camp in 2018.

completed six of 15 passes for 74 yards as the Bills were blown out by the Ravens.

The Bills decided to give Allen the starting job the next week. They lost at home to the Chargers. But he did throw his first career touchdown pass.

Allen had his breakout game the next week. The Bills went on the road to play the Minnesota Vikings. Nobody expected the Bills to win. But Allen led a dominant first half. He threw for a touchdown and ran for two more. On one run, he leaped over Anthony Barr, Minnesota's 6-foot-5-inch linebacker. The play got Allen a lot of attention on social media. The Bills went on to win the game 27–6.

Allen went viral when he hurdled Minnesota's Anthony Barr during his rookie season.

PROVING IT ON THE FIELD

Choosing Allen seventh overall in the draft came as a surprise to some people. One of them was cornerback Jalen Ramsey of the Jaguars. Ramsey called Allen "trash" and believed other quarterbacks should have been taken ahead of him. Allen let his play do the talking. He and the Bills beat Ramsey and the Jaguars in 2018.

Any NFL rookie has highs and lows. Allen was no different. He followed the Vikings game with a clunker. Allen was sacked seven times and threw two interceptions in a shutout loss at Green Bay. The next week, Allen led his first fourth-quarter comeback as the Bills beat the Titans on a last-second field goal. But a week later, Allen hurt his elbow and had to leave the game. The injury sidelined him for a month.

Allen returned for the final six games of the season. The Bills won half of them. He closed the season with his best game yet. Allen passed

Allen had a hand in five touchdowns as the Bills blew out Miami in 2018.

for three touchdowns and ran for two more in a blowout win over Miami.

The Bills finished just 6–10. But they were 5–6 with Allen as a starter. That gave Buffalo fans reason for hope.

4 PLAYOFF QUARTERBACK

Allen was quickly becoming a leader for the Bills. He was named a team captain for the 2019 season. That was unusual for just a second-year player. Buffalo hoped to compete for a playoff spot in 2019.

But the season opener against the New York Jets started out as bad as could be. Allen lost a fumble on the first drive of the game. Then he threw an interception that was returned for a touchdown. He lost

Allen led a huge comeback win over the Jets in the first game of 2019.

Allen celebrates his Thanksgiving Day victory over the Dallas Cowboys in 2019.

another fumble and threw another interception before the half was over.

Buffalo trailed 16–3 in the fourth quarter. Suddenly Allen came alive. He ran for a touchdown early in the quarter. When the Bills got the ball back, he drove them 80 yards in eight plays. Allen hit John Brown for a 38-yard touchdown to put the Bills on top for good. On those two touchdown drives, Allen went 8-for-10 for 103 yards. It wasn't always pretty, but Allen got the job done.

The Bills started 3–0. After a loss to New England, Allen threw two touchdown passes in each of the next three games. Then a three-game winning streak in November left the Bills 9–3 on the season. That included an easy 26–15 win over Dallas on Thanksgiving Day. Allen completed 19 of 24 passes for 231 yards and a touchdown. Allen was showing off his accuracy, and the Bills were winning.

TWO JOSH ALLENS

Despite being a relatively common name, there was only one Josh Allen in the NFL before the 2018 season. Then suddenly there were two at once. The Jaguars selected Josh Allen the linebacker seventh overall in the 2019 draft. That was the same spot where the Bills took Josh Allen the quarterback in 2018.

Allen helped the Bills rally and force overtime against the Texans.

Buffalo had a shot at its first division title since 1995. A late-season loss to New England ended those hopes. But the Bills still made the playoffs.

Looking for their first playoff win in 24 years, the Bills traveled to Houston to face the Texans. The game started like a reverse of the season opener. This time the Bills started hot. Allen scored on a touchdown pass on the offense's first drive. But he didn't throw the pass. He caught it on a trick play.

Buffalo built a 16–0 lead midway through the third quarter. But then it all unraveled. The Texans scored 19 straight points. The Bills had one more chance. The ball was at their own 30. They had no timeouts left and 1:16 on the clock. Allen came up with a long run and two big third-down passes to keep the drive alive. Buffalo tied it with a field goal to force overtime.

The Bills had one possession in overtime to win the game, but they ended up punting. Houston drove deep into Buffalo territory and kicked a game-winning field goal.

Though 2019 ended in disappointment, it was still a big step forward. Allen showed he could make the Bills winners again. Fans were excited to see what he could do next.

TRICK PLAY

Allen got to try his hand at receiver in the 2019 playoff game against the Houston Texans. His 16-yard touchdown catch gave the Bills an early 7–0 lead.

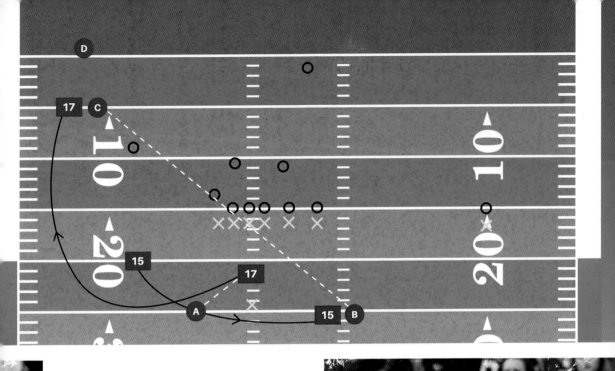

HOW IT HAPPENED

From the 16-yard line, Allen (17) takes the snap and pitches it to Brown (15), who is cutting behind him (A). Brown continues to his right as Allen slips out of the backfield and runs down the left sideline. Brown stops at the 26-yard line (B) and throws back across the field to Allen, who catches it at the 5-yard line (C). Allen takes two steps and dives into the end zone for the touchdown (D).

TIMELINE

1. ## Firebaugh, California (May 21, 1996)
   Josh Allen is born.

2. ## Reedley, California (2014)
   Allen enrolls at Reedley College after receiving no scholarship offers from major college football programs.

3. ## Laramie, Wyoming (September 5, 2015)
   After receiving a scholarship offer from the University of Wyoming, Allen makes his college debut with the Cowboys.

4. ## Boise, Idaho (December 22, 2017)
   Allen makes his final college start in the Famous Idaho Potato Bowl.

5. ## Arlington, Texas (April 26, 2018)
   The Buffalo Bills select Allen with the seventh pick in the NFL Draft.

6. ## Buffalo, New York (September 16, 2018)
   Allen makes his first NFL start against the Los Angeles Chargers.

7. ## Pittsburgh, Pennsylvania (December 15, 2019)
   Allen and the Bills clinch a playoff spot by defeating the Pittsburgh Steelers on *Sunday Night Football*.

8. ## Houston, Texas (January 4, 2020)
   Allen makes his first career playoff start, a 22-19 overtime loss to the Houston Texans.

MAP

Birth date: May 21, 1996

Birthplace:
Firebaugh, California

Position: Quarterback

Throws: Right

Height: 6 feet 5 inches

Weight: 237 pounds

Current team: Buffalo Bills
(2018–)

Past teams: Reedley College
Tigers (2014), Wyoming
Cowboys (2015–17)

Major awards: AFC Offensive Player of the Week (2018 Week 17,
2019 Week 11), Famous Idaho Potato Bowl Most Valuable Player
(2017)

Accurate through the 2019 NFL season and playoffs.

GLOSSARY

blowout
Decided by a large margin; lopsided.

breakout
A notable performance early in one's career that shows promise for the future.

coordinator
An assistant coach who is in charge of the offense or defense.

draft
A system that allows teams to acquire new players coming into a league.

drive
A series of plays in which one team has the ball.

junior college
A two-year college that often includes athletic programs.

rookie
A first-year player.

sacked
Tackled behind the line of scrimmage while attempting to pass.

scholarship
Money awarded to a student to pay for education expenses.

trick play
A play designed to fool the other team.

TO LEARN MORE

Books

Hunter, Tony. *Buffalo Bills*. Minneapolis, MN: Abdo Publishing, 2020.

Whiting, Jim. *Buffalo Bills*. Mankato, MN: Creative Education, 2019.

York, Andy. *Ultimate College Football Road Trip*. Minneapolis, MN: Abdo Publishing, 2019.

Websites

Buffalo Bills
www.buffalobills.com

Josh Allen College Stats
www.sports-reference.com/cfb/players/josh-allen-7.html

Josh Allen Pro Stats
www.pro-football-reference.com/players/A/AlleJo02.htm

INDEX